Louise Chandler Moulton

In the Garden of Dreams

Lyrics and Sonnets

Louise Chandler Moulton

In the Garden of Dreams
Lyrics and Sonnets

ISBN/EAN: 9783743311886

Manufactured in Europe, USA, Canada, Australia, Japa

Cover: Foto ©Thomas Meinert / pixelio.de

Manufactured and distributed by brebook publishing software (www.brebook.com)

Louise Chandler Moulton

In the Garden of Dreams

TABLE OF CONTENTS.

Lyrics.

	PAGE
COME BACK, DEAR DAYS	11
LOVE'S RESURRECTION DAY	13
THE STRENGTH OF THE HILLS	14
"IF THERE WERE DREAMS TO SELL"	16
IN THE RANKS	18
EROS	19
LAUS VENERIS	20
PARLEYING	22
IN BOHEMIA	23
TO NIGHT	24
WHEN DAY WAS DONE	25
MAUD'S ROSES	27
"THEIR CANDLES ARE ALL OUT"	28
TO MISTRESS ROSE	30
AT MIDNIGHT	31
IN A BOWER	33
ROSES	34
THE GHOST'S RETURN	35
AS I SAIL	37
A GIRL'S FUNERAL IN MILAN	39

TABLE OF CONTENTS.

	PAGE
In a Garden	40
At End	42
The Coquette's Defence	43
Do not Grieve	45
Old Jones is Dead	46
Grandmamma's Warning	48
Maid Marion	49
A Little Comedy	51
In Autumn	53
At Five o'Clock	54
Beside a Bier	55
Red and White Roses	56
My Saint	57
Warning	58
The Rose she wore in Winter	59
Shall not know?	60
For a Birthday	62
A Mood of Love	63
Nay	64
The Roses of La Garraye	65
Now and Then	67
"The King is Dead, Long Live the King!"	68

Sonnets in Many Moods.

Helen's Cup	73
Silent Sorrow	74
A Cry	75
Love's Empty House	76
After Death	77

TABLE OF CONTENTS.

	PAGE
VOICES ON THE WIND	78
THE CUP OF DEATH	79
TO A MODERN POET	80
THE LAST GOOD-BY	81
LOVE IS DEAD	82
HIC JACET	83
LEFT BEHIND	84
FUTURE FORGIVENESS	85
IN PACE	86
A WOMAN'S KNOWLEDGE	87
IN SOLITUDE	88
BEYOND SIGHT AND SOUND	89
TO ONE WHO HAS LOVED OFTEN	90
BEFORE THE SHRINE	91
ROSES AT SEA	92
A GHOST'S QUESTION	93
SISTER SORROW	94
HE LOVED	95
HEREAFTER	96
AT WAR	97
NEAR, YET FAR	98
A FALLEN HOUSE	99
MY MOURNER	100
AT SEA	101
LAURA SLEEPING	102
TO ONE MOST UNHAPPY	103
IN THE COURT OF THE LIONS	104
MY CASTLE	105
BY MARCH WIND LED	106
MY MOTHER'S PICTURE	107
AT A RUINED ABBEY	108

His Second Wife Speaks.

	Page
I. A Parable	113
II. Silent	114
III. A Second Place	115
IV. Alone in Death	116
V. Face to Face	117

The Still Hour.

In the Pine Woods at Marienbad	121
Help Thou my Unbelief!	122
Shall I look back?	123
Straight on to Port	124
A Prayer in Sorrow	125
On Homeward Wing	126
In Mid-ocean	127
As in Vision	128
A Prayer for Light	129
Come unto Me	130
A Rainy Afternoon	131
Hark, Ten Thousand Harps and Voices!	132

Rosemary.

Ralph Waldo Emerson	137
An Open Door	138
Behind the Mist	139
Her Ghost	140
At End of Pain	143
A Silent Guest	144
Louisa M. Alcott	145

To French Tunes.

RONDELS.

	PAGE
The Spring is here	149
Easter Sunday	150
Heart, Sad Heart	151
Two Red Roses	152
The Shadow-dance	153
In February	154
The Old Beau	155
To John Greenleaf Whittier	156

RONDEAUX.

"With those Clear Eyes"	157
Love's Ghost	158
How could I tell?	159
When Love was young	160
If Love could last	161
O Sweetest Maid!	162
If you were here	163

TRIOLETS.

Such Joy it was	164
We loved so well	165
So blithely rose	166
Thistle-down	167
Love plumes his Wings	168

BALLADE.

In Winter	169

ILLUSTRATIONS.

*The designs by H. Winthrop Peirce.
Engraved by John Andrew and Son Co., Boston.*

	PAGE
LUTE AND FLUTE AND MINSTRELSY	10
"BURSTING BUDS THAT JUNES UNFOLD"	11
LOVE'S RESURRECTION DAY	13
TELEMACHUS	73
TINTERN ABBEY	109
"BUT OMINOUSLY THROUGH THOSE HALLS THERE FELL STRANGE SOUNDS AS OF OLD MUSIC IN THE AIR"	112
LILY AND STAR	120
THE STILL HOUR	121
LIGHT	133
ROSEMARY	137
MEMORY	146
THE SINGER	148
L'AMOUR DU RONDEAU	171

Lyrics.

'T is my delight alone in summer shade
To pipe a simple song for thinking hearts.
WORDSWORTH.

COME BACK, DEAR DAYS.

COME back, dear days, from out the past!
   . . . I see your gentle ghosts arise;
  You look at me with mournful eyes,
And then the night grows vague and vast:
  You have gone back to Paradise.

Why did you fleet away, dear days?
  You were so welcome when you came!
  The morning skies were all aflame;
The birds sang matins in your praise;
  All else of life you put to shame.

Did I not honor you aright, —
  I, who but lived to see you shine,
  Who felt your very pain divine,
Thanked God and warmed me in your light,
  Or quaffed your tears as they were wine?

What wooed you to those stranger skies,—
    What love more fond, what dream more fair,
    What music whispered in the air?
What soft delight of smiles and sighs
    Enchanted you from otherwhere?

You left no pledges when you went:
    The years since then are bleak and cold;
    No bursting buds the Junes unfold.
While you were here my all I spent;
    Now I am poor and sad and old.

LOVE'S RESURRECTION DAY.

ROUND among the quiet graves,
    When the sun was low,
Love went grieving, — Love who saves:
    Did the sleepers know?

At his touch the flowers awoke,
    At his tender call
Birds into sweet singing broke,
    And it did befall

From the blooming, bursting sod
    All Love's dead arose,
And went flying up to God
    By a way Love knows.

THE STRENGTH OF THE HILLS.

FOR L. I. G.

MY thoughts go home to that old brown house
    With its low roof sloping down to the east,
And its garden fragrant with roses and thyme
That blossom no longer except in rhyme,
    Where the honey-bees used to feast.

Afar in the west the great hills rose,
    Silent and steadfast and gloomy and gray:
I thought they were giants, and doomed to keep
Their watch while the world should wake or sleep,
    Till the trumpet should sound on the judgment day.

I used to wonder of what they dreamed
    As they brooded there in their silent might,
While March winds smote them, or June rains fell,
Or the snows of winter their ghostly spell
    Wrought in the long and lonesome night.

They remembered a younger world than ours,
    Before the trees on their top were born,
When the old brown house was itself a tree,
And waste were the fields where now you see
    The winds astir in the tasselled corn.

And I was as young as the hills were old,
   And the world was warm with the breath of spring,
And the roses red and the lilies white
Budded and bloomed for my heart's delight,
   And the birds in my heart began to sing.

But calm in the distance the great hills rose,
   Deaf unto rapture and dumb unto pain,
Since they knew that Joy is the mother of Grief,
And remembered a butterfly's life is brief,
   And the sun sets only to rise again.

They will brood and dream and be silent as now,
   When the youngest children alive to-day
Have grown to be women and men, — grown old,
And gone from the world like a tale that is told,
   And even whose echo forgets to stay.

"IF THERE WERE DREAMS TO SELL."

> *If there were dreams to sell,*
> *What would you buy?*
>   BEDDOES.

IF there were dreams to sell,
 Do I not know full well
  What I would buy?
Hope's dear delusive spell
Its happy tale to tell,
  Joy's fleeting sigh.

I would be young again:
Youth's madding bliss and bane
  I would recapture;
Though it were keen with pain,
All else seems void and vain
  To that fine rapture.

I would be glad once more,
Slip through an open door
  Into Life's glory;
Keep what I spent of yore,
Find what I lost before,
  Hear an old story.

As it one day befell,
Breaking Death's frozen spell,
    Love should draw nigh:
If there were dreams to sell,
Do I not know too well
    What I would buy?

IN THE RANKS.

HIS death-blow struck him there in the ranks, —
    There in the ranks, with his face to the foe:
Did his dying lips utter curses or thanks?
                No one will know.

Still he marched on, he with the rest, —
    Still he marched on, with his face to the foe,
To the day's bitter business sternly addressed:
                Dead — did they know?

When the day was over, the fierce fight done,
    His cheeks were red with the sunset's glow;
And they crowned him there with their laurels won:
                Dead — did he know?

Laurels or roses, all one to him now:
    What to a dead man is glory or glow?
Rose wreaths for love, or a crown on his brow:
                Dead — does he know?

And yet you will see him march on with the rest, —
    No man of them all makes a goodlier show, —
In the thick of the tumult jostled and pressed:
                Dead — would you know?

EROS.

FILL the swift days full, my dear,
    Since life is fleet;
Love, and hold Love fast, my dear,
    He is so sweet —
Sweetest, dearest, fleetest comer,
Fledgling of the sudden summer.

Love, but not too well, my dear!
    When skies are gray,
And the autumn winds are here,
    Love will away —
Fleetest, vaguest, farthest rover
When the summer's warmth is over.

LAUS VENERIS:

A PICTURE BY BURNE JONES.

PALLID with too much longing,
    White with passion and prayer,
Goddess of love and beauty,
    She sits in the picture there,—

Sits with her dark eyes seeking
    Something more subtle still
Than the old delights of loving
    Her measureless days to fill.

She has loved and been loved so often
    In her long, immortal years,
That she tires of the worn-out rapture,
    Sickens of hopes and fears.

No joys or sorrows move her,
    Done with her ancient pride;
For her head she found too heavy
    The crown she has cast aside.

Clothed in her scarlet splendor,
    Bright with her glory of hair,
Sad that she is not mortal,—
    Eternally sad and fair,

Longing for joys she knows not,
    Athirst with a vain desire,
There she sits in the picture,
    Daughter of foam and fire.

PARLEYING.

I HOLD a shadow's cold, soft hand,
　　I look in eyes you cannot see,
And words you cannot understand
Come back, as from a distant land, —
　　The far-off land of Memory.

Forgive me that I sit apart
　　And hold the shadow's hand in mine,
The past broods darkly in my heart,
And bitter are the tears that start;
　　I would not mix them with the wine.

The hour will pass: the shade will go
　　To his dark home, and swift forget,
At rest the daisied turf below,
The sun-warmed hours we used to know,
　　And the old paths wherein we met.

I am alive! Why should the dead
　　With cold hand hold the quick in thrall?
To his far place the shade has sped,
Now Life with Life may gayly wed!
　　. . . My heart misgives me, after all.

IN BOHEMIA.

I CAME between the glad green hills,
   Whereon the summer sunshine lay,
  And all the world was young that day,
As when the Spring's soft laughter thrills
   The pulses of the waking May —
You were alive — yet scarce I knew
The world was glad because of you.

I came between the sad green hills,
   Whereon the summer twilight lay,
  And all the world was old that day,
And hoary age forgets the thrills
   That woke the pulses of the May —
And you were dead — too well I knew
The world was sad because of you.

TO NIGHT.

BEND low, O dusky Night,
    And give my spirit rest;
  Hold me to your deep breast,
And put old cares to flight;
Give back the lost delight
    That once my soul possessed,
    When Love was loveliest, —
Bend low, O dusky Night!

Enfold me in your arms, —
    The sole embrace I crave
    Until the embracing grave
Shield me from life's alarms.
I dare your subtlest charms;
    Your deepest spell I brave, —
    O, strong to slay or save,
Enfold me in your arms!

WHEN DAY WAS DONE.

FOR L. W.

THE clouds that watched in the west have fled;
    The sun has set and the moon is high;
And nothing is left of the day that is dead
    Save a fair white ghost in the eastern sky.

While the day was dying we knelt and yearned,
    And hoped and prayed till its last breath died;
But since to a radiant ghost it has turned,
    Shall we rest with that white grace satisfied?

The fair ghost smiles with a pale, cold smile,
    As mocking as life and as hopeless as death —
Shall passionless beauty like this beguile?
    Who loves a ghost without feeling or breath?

I remember a maiden as fair to see,
    Who once was alive, with a heart like June;
She died, but her spirit wanders free,
    And charms men's souls to the old mad tune.

Warm she was, in her life's glad day, —
    Warm and fair, and faithful and sweet;
A man might have thrown a kingdom away
    To kneel and love at her girlish feet.

But the night came down, and her day was done;
    Hoping and dreaming were over for aye;
And then her career as a ghost was begun —
    Cold she shone, like the moon on high.

For maiden or moon shall a live man yearn?
    Shall a breathing man love a ghost without
        breath?
Shine, moon, and chill us, you cannot burn;
    Go home, Girl-Ghost, to your kingdom of death.

MAUD'S ROSES.

ALONE all day in my cabin,
   With never a mortal to see,
I look at Maud's delicate roses,
   And the roses look at me.

Like her they are fair and stately;
   Like her they are proud and sweet;
And their hue seems made of her blushes,
   Where the roses and lilies meet.

And what is their subtle fragrance
   But the love that she bade them tell,
Or the breath she breathed through their petals
   When she lingered to say farewell?

Ah! roses that stayed when she vanished,
   Ah! roses that smile, though she went,
How you mock at the sadness of parting,
   With your passionless, perfect content!

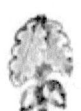

"THEIR CANDLES ARE ALL OUT."

FOR L. C. B.

WHAT hap dismays the dead? Their couch is low;
  And over it the summer grasses creep,
  Or winter snows enshroud it, white and deep,
Or long-prevailing winds of autumn blow.

They hear no rumor of our joy or woe:
  The ways we tread are perilous and steep;
  They climb no longer, free at last to sleep,
Our weariful, vexed life no more to know.

Do they forget their loves of long ago,
  And the glad hopes that made their glad hearts leap?
  Or the spent joys for which they used to weep,
When Love and Sorrow buffeted them so?

On us, by winds of Fate swept to and fro,
  Do they have pity, whom no rude winds sweep?
  How can I tell? Their mystery they keep,
Beneath the blossoms as beneath the snow.

And yet, I think, from that deep rest below,
  They would be glad to rise and love and weep;
  Once more the thankless harvest field to reap
Of human joy and pain, — life's whole to know.

TO MISTRESS ROSE.

A ROSE by any other name?
    Nay, that could hardly be.
No other name, my Flower of June,
    Could be the name for thee.

Dear darling of the summer-time
    And love-child of the sun,
Whether by thy sweet breath beguiled
    Or by thy thorns undone,

I know thee for the Queen of Flowers,
    And toast thee by thy name, —
" Here 's to the sweet young loveliness
    That sets our hearts aflame ! "

AT MIDNIGHT.

THE room is cold and dark to-night:
    The fire is low, —
Why come you, you who love the light,
    To mock me so?

I pray you leave me now alone;
    You worked your will,
And turned my heart to frozen stone, —
    Why haunt me still?

I got me to this empty place;
    I shut the door, —
Yet through the dark I see your face
    Just as of yore.

The old smile curves your lips to-night;
    Your deep eyes glow
With that old gleam that made them bright
    So long ago.

I listen: do I hear your tone
    The silence thrill?
Why come you? I would be alone;
    Why vex me still?

What! Would you that we re-embrace, —
    We two once more?
Are these your tears that wet my face
    Just as before?

You left to seek some new delight,
    Yet your tears flow;
What sorrow brings you back to-night?
    Shall I not know?

I will not let you grieve alone, —
    The night is chill, —
Though love is dead and hope has flown,
    Pity lives still.

    .   .   .   .   .

How silent is the empty space!
    Dreamed I once more?
Henceforth against your haunting face
    I bar the door.

IN A BOWER.

A MAIDEN sits in her bower and sings,
    And your heart keeps time to the tune ;
In the garden walks the red rose springs, —
        The month is June.

The month is June, and full are the days, —
    Fair days, of the summer fed ;
And softly the singer sings her lays :
        Her lips are red.

A face she has that is pale as Sleep,
    And hair like the midnight skies
When the wings of tempest across them sweep,
        And strange dark eyes.

The song she sings is a siren's song,
    A tempting, dangerous rune, —
If you hark at all you will hear too long
        That fatal tune.

ROSES.

ROSES that briefly live,
    Joy is your dower;
Blest be the Fates that give
    One perfect hour.
And, though too soon you die,
    In your dust glows
Something the passer-by
    Knows was a Rose.

THE GHOST'S RETURN.

BACK through the rain and mist
    Of my far way,
I have come, whom you kissed
    That other day.

See, love, I wait outside
    While the rains fall:
Through the night, void and wide,
    Hark to my call.

Do you falter, you who loved
    So long and well,
Now I my love have proved,
    Breaking Death's spell?

Leaving those pale delights
    Dead folk that thrill,
Through their dim days and nights,
    Wait I your will.

Dear love, unbar the door,
    Life is so sweet!
Warmed on your heart once more,
    My heart shall beat.

Snatch me from very Death:
　　Heaven will forgive.
Breathe in my lips your breath:
　　Then I shall live.

Nay, but you shrink with fear,
　　No welcome speak, —
Now shall the grave be dear,
　　Love is so weak.

AS I SAIL.

FAR on the gray sea glooms and glowers,
    Far off the salt winds vaguely stray,
And through the long monotonous hours
    My thoughts go wandering on their way;

Go back to find that earlier time
    When, lingering by a bluer sea,
A poet wooed me with his rhyme,
    And all the world was changed for me.

The winds to music strange were set,
    The sunsets glowed with sudden flame,
And all the shining sands were wet
    With waves that whispered as they came,

And told a tender low-breathed tale
    Of love that always should be young;
Dear love that should not change or fail, —
    Such love as love-lorn bards have sung.

Pale roses bloomed by that far sea,
    And shivered at the sea-wind's breath;
A bird flew low, and sang to me —
    "The end of love and life is death."

I left the pale rose where it grew;
    I would not heed the warning bird;
Of all the world I, only, knew
    How sweet the music I had heard, —

How dear the love, how true the truth
    My poet uttered in his rhyme;
And how it gave me back my youth
    In that deep-hearted summer-time.

Then winter came; the pale rose died,
    And to the south the wise bird flew;
And I — ah me, the world is wide,
    And poets love while love is new.

A GIRL'S FUNERAL IN MILAN.

THERE in the strange old gilded hearse
    With a mound of paper-flowers on her breast,
Her life being over, for better or worse,
    They bore her on to her final rest.

And the women followed her, two by two,
    And talked of how young she was to die;
And the cold drops drenched them through and
    through,
    As under the pitiless, frowning sky

On they marched in the drizzling rain
    To the little old church in the Milan square,
Where the choir-boys chanted with shrill refrain,
    And the toothless Padre muttered his prayer;

Then straight to the waiting grave they went;
    And the rain rained on, and the wind was still;
Since, all her treasure of life being spent,
    It was time Death had of the girl his will.

And they left her there with the rain and the wind,
    Glad, I think, to have come to the end;
For the grave folds close, and the sod is kind,
    And thus do the friendless find a friend.

IN A GARDEN.

PALE in the pallid moonlight,
    White as the rose on her breast,
She stood in the fair Rose-garden
    With her shy young love confessed.

The roses climbed to kiss her,
    The violets, purple and sweet,
Breathed their despair in the fragrance
    That bathed her beautiful feet.

She stood there, stately and slender,
    Gold hair on her shoulders shed,
Clothed all in white, like the visions
    When the living behold the dead.

There, with her lover beside her,
    With life and with love she thrilled —
What mattered the world's wide sorrow
    To her with her joy fulfilled?

Next year, in the fair Rose-garden,
    He waited, alone and dumb,
If perchance from the silent country
    The soul of the dead would come,

To comfort the living and loving
    With the ghost of a lost delight,
And thrill into quivering welcome
    The desolate, brooding night:

Till softly a wind from the distance
    Began to blow and blow;
The moon bent nearer and nearer,
    And, solemn and sweet and slow,

Came a wonderful rapture of music
    That turned to her voice, at last:
Then a cold, soft touch on his forehead,
    Like the breath of the wind that passed,—

Like the breath of the wind she touched him;
    Thin was her voice and cold;
And something that seemed like a shadow
    Slipped through his feverish hold:

But the voice had said, "I love you,
    With my first love and my last"—
Then again that wonderful music,
    And he knew that her soul had passed.

AT END.

At end of Love, at end of Life,
　　At end of Hope, at end of Strife,
At end of all we cling to so —
The sun is setting — must we go?

At dawn of Love, at dawn of Life,
At dawn of Peace that follows Strife,
At dawn of all we long for so —
The sun is rising — let us go!

THE COQUETTE'S DEFENCE.

RED, red roses glowing in the garden,
    Rare, white lilies swaying on your stalks,
Did you hear me pray my sweet love for pardon,
    Straying with him through your garden walks?

Ah, *you* glow and smile when the sun shines upon
    you —
    You thrill with delight at the tears of the dew,
And the wind that caresses you boasts that he won
    you —
    Do you think, fair flowers, to them all to be true?

Sun, dew, and wind, ah, they all are your lovers —
    Sun, dew, and wind, and you love them back
    again —
And you flirt with the idle, white moth that hovers
    Above your sweet beauty, and laugh at his pain.

Must I, then, be deaf to the wooers that love me,
    And because I can hear should my sweet Love
    complain?
Does he not, in forgiving me, stand high above me,
    And punish my fault with his gentle disdain?

You trifle, fair flowers, with the many, but one lord
  Wooes you, and wins you, and conquers the
    throng :
Dews and winds cool you, for warmth you turn sun-
    ward, —
  You know and I know to whom we belong.

DO NOT GRIEVE.

I WOULD not have you mourn too much,
   When I am lying low,—
Your grief would grieve me even then,
   Should your tears flow.

But only plant above my grave
   One little sprig of rue;
Then find yourself a fairer love,
   But not more true.

The summer winds will come and go
   Above me as I lie;
And if I think at all, my dear,
   As they pass by,

I shall remember the old love,
   With all its bliss and bane, —
Though Life nor Death can bring me back
   The old, sweet pain.

OLD JONES IS DEAD.

I SAT in my window, high overhead,
   And heard them say, below in the street,
"I suppose you know that old Jones is dead?"
   Then the speakers passed, and I heard their feet
Heedlessly walking their onward way, —
"Dead!" what more could there be to say?

But I sat and pondered what it might mean
   Thus to be dead while the world went by:
Did Jones see farther than we have seen?
   Was he one with the stars in the watching sky?
Or down there under the growing grass
Did he hear the feet of the daylight pass?

Were daytime and night-time as one to him now,
   And grieving and hoping a tale that is told?
A kiss on his lips, or a hand on his brow,
   Could he feel them under the church-yard mould,
As he surely had felt them his whole life long,
Though they passed with his youth-time, hot and
     strong?

They called him " Old Jones " when at last he died ;
　" Old Jones " he had been for many a year ;
Yet his faithful memory Time defied,
　And dwelt in the days so distant and dear,
When first he had found that love was sweet
And recked not the speed of its hurrying feet.

Does he brood, in the long night under the sod,
　On the joys and sorrows he used to know ;
Or far in some wonderful world of God,
　Where the shining seraphs stand, row on row,
Does he wake like a child at the daylight's gleam,
And know that the past was a night's short dream?

Is he dead, and a clod there, down below ;
　Or dead and wiser than any alive ;
Which?　Ah, who of us all may know,
　Or who can say how the dead folk thrive?—
But the summer morning is cool and sweet,
And I hear the live folk laugh in the street.

GRANDMAMMA'S WARNING.

"LOVE is a fire," she said. "Love is a fire,
　　Beware the madness of that wild desire!
I know, for I was young, and now am old" ....
"Oh, did you learn by what your elders told?"

MAID MARION.

LITTLE Maid Marion, Rose in June,
   What breath of prophecy comes and goes,
And stirs your heart like a vagrant tune
   Till the deepening bloom on your soft cheek glows,

And your blue eyes shine like the morning sky
   Just alight with the morning star —
Hopeful and happy and sweet and shy,
   While day and its glare are yet afar?

Have you heard a name that we do not hear
   And set it to music all your own?
Has there come to you in a vision, Dear,
   A face that only your eyes have known?

Or is it still but a wandering voice
   That whispers you something vague and sweet,
Of days of wooing and days of choice,
   And hearts that meet as the waters meet?

Days that will come to you, Rose in June —
   Days that will test you and try you and show
The sacredest meaning, the secretest tune,
   Of all that your maidenly heart can know.

They will leave you not as they find you, Dear —
    The morning star gives place to the sun;
But your blue eyes meet me, faithful and clear,
    I can trust your soul, when the dream is done.

A LITTLE COMEDY.

IS the world the same, do you think, my dear,
    As when we walked by the sea together,
And the white caps danced and the cliffs rose sheer,
    And we were glad in the autumn weather?

You played at loving that day, my dear, —
    How well you told me that tender story, —
And I made answer, with smile and tear,
    While the sky was flushed with the sunset's glory.

Now I shut my eyes, and I see, my dear,
    That far-off path by the surging ocean, —
I shut my eyes, and I seem to hear
    Your voice surmounting the tide's commotion.

It was but a comedy slight, my dear. —
    Why should its memory come to vex me?
Can it be I am longing that you should appear
    And play it again? My thoughts perplex me.

'T is the sea and the shore that I miss, my dear, —
    The sea and the shore, and the sunset's glory:
Or would these be nothing without you near,
    To murmur again that fond, old story?

I know you now but too well, my dear, —
    With your heart as light as a wind-blown feather, —
Yet somehow the world seems cold and drear
    Without your acting, this autumn weather.

IN AUTUMN.

WITH the leaves around her dying,
    And the wind around her sighing,
And her listless hands together,
She sits in the autumn weather.

The sad little streams are grieving,
The poor little birds are leaving,
And the flowers and she together
Fade in the autumn weather.

AT FIVE O'CLOCK.

TO K. F. POURING TEA.

FAIR Lady Rose, round whom black-coated bees
    Make murmurous humming all the afternoon, —
Thou dost belong to the soft, summer ease
Of purple islands, where the southern seas
    Break on the shore with soft beguiling rune.

Lands fair as the far-famed Hesperides
    Should be thy home, O Lady of the June!
And thou shouldst pour, instead of cups like these,
Some magic draught, which to the subtle lees
    Thy slaves should quaff, and praise thee all in tune

To playing of such melodies as please
    Fair ladies' ears, and win for Love love's boon :
And sweet, beneath the gently-drooping trees,
Should be the tender whisper of the breeze,
    And time should pause for thee at golden noon.

BESIDE A BIER.

I HAD never kissed her her whole life long,—
   Now I stand by her bier does she feel
How, with love that the waiting years made strong,
   I set on her lips my seal?

Will she wear my kiss in the grave's long night,
   And wake sometimes with a thrill
From dreams of the old life's missed delight,
   To feel that the grave is chill?

"It was warm," will she say, "in that world above :
   It was warm, but I did not know
How he loved me there, with his whole life's love—
   It is cold, down here below."

RED AND WHITE ROSES.

ROSES the lover gives to his love;
    Roses we lay on the breast of death
That nevermore fondest whisper can move,—
Which is the sweeter, answer and prove,
    Passionate love, or sleep without breath?

For love you burn with a crimson fire,
    For death you are pale as the winter's snow:
Warm for the one, with the heart's desire,
Cold for the other, since hopes expire,—
    Which is the sweeter? When shall we know?

MY SAINT.

OH long the weary vigils since you left me, —
    In your far home, I wonder, can you know
To what dread uttermost your loss bereft me,
    Or half it meant to me that you should go?

This world is full, indeed, of fair hopes perished,
    And loves more fleet than this poor fleeting breath;
But that deep heart in which my heart was cherished
    Must surely have survived what we call Death.

They cannot cease — our own true dead — to love us,
    And you will hear this far-off cry of mine,
Though you keep holiday so high above us,
    Where all the happy spirits sing and shine.

Steal back to me to-night, from your far dwelling,
    Beyond the pilgrim moon, beyond the sun:
They will not miss your single voice for swelling
    Their rapture-chorus — you are only one.

Ravish my soul, as with divine embraces;
    Teach me, if Life is false, that Death is true;
With pledge of new delights in heavenly places
    Entice my spirit, — take me hence with you!

WARNING.

Fly away, O white-winged moth!
    Wherefore burn your tender wings?
Fatal is the flame you love
    To such gauzy things.

That too ardent crimson ray
    Only steel may safely prove:
Use your wings to fly away —
    You're too slight for love.

THE ROSE SHE WORE IN WINTER.

TO R. H.

O ROSE, so subtly sweet!
   What dost thou in the snow —
The time of frost and sleet,
   When roses should not blow —
   Playing at summer so?

When we that beauty meet,
   Which nightingales in June
For love and bliss entreat,
   With what cold, wintry rune
   Shall we thy praise entune?

My Rose, so subtly sweet,
   Thy rose-red lips I kiss;
I kneel at thy dear feet,
   Dear Rose, and do not miss
   The summer's by-gone bliss.

SHALL I NOT KNOW?

WHEN over me the heedless wild things grow,
    Will any mourn for me a little space,
Or grieve that in that grave so cool and low
    I find my resting-place?

The strong world will go on though I am still,
    The morning sun mock darkness with his pride,
The sunset splendors clothe the western hill,
    As though I had not died.

The spring flowers will awake in field and hedge,
    And summer roses answer to the sun;
The lone, last bird wail in the icy sedge
    For winter's reign begun;

And loves, like summer blossoms, burst to bloom
    And sweeten with their fragrance all the air,
And hates grow strong, like weeds about a tomb,
    While I am silent there.

No fleeting joys shall mock me where I lie;
    No hate so keen that it can pierce that rest:
I shall not hear Life's footsteps passing by,
    Or know that Death is best.

Yet, shouldst thou come, when all the stars are bright
    And all the sky by their cold light possest,
And hark to hear, through voices of the night,
    Her voice who loved thee best,

Perchance, though I were frozen in the grave,
    My heart might quicken when it heard thy call,
And even then strong Love be strong to save —
    Love who is lord of all:

Or if, sealed fast by Death, even to that cry
    My ears were deaf and my closed lips were dumb,
My soul, heedless of others passing by,
    Might know that Thou hadst come.

For me the busy world will not stand still,
    Nor in one heart the summer cease to glow;
And Love and Life on earth shall have their will:
    But, come! shall I not know?

FOR A BIRTHDAY.

M. B. A.

THRICE happy day, that saw our Fair Maid's eyes
    First open to the sunshine! Art thou come
To see if yet the light of Paradise
    Has faded from them, in her earthly home?

Nay, there it shines! As innocent and true
    As that first day, she dwells among us yet;
Look in those eyes of Heaven's serenest blue,
    And see the Heaven she never can forget.

A MOOD OF LOVE.

Do I love thee? Who can tell?
    Time was when I loved thee well:
Is this love that now I bear,
Or does Use Love's semblance wear?

Should I grieve if thou wert gone?
Should I miss thee, left alone?
Would the summer be less sweet
If our lips should never meet?

If some other fairer Fair
Fettered thee with silken snare,
Should I sorrow to behold
Thee her captive — mine of old?

Ah, it may be, should we part,
I should learn how dear thou art, —
When the gods withdraw we know
How divine the feet that go.

NAY.

SHALL we grow old together?
    Nay! though 'tis wintry weather
The earth awaits the spring,
When suns shall warm the heather,
When birds will moult and feather,
    And happy things take wing:
And thou and I together,
Defying wintry weather,
    We, too, will wait our spring.

THE ROSES OF LA GARRAYE.

AMONG the ruins of La Garraye
   Grow wonderful roses, as pale as death,—
  Roses that never a fervid breath
Of the Breton summer glad and gay
Can warm with a single crimson ray.

Mid ruins and roses two lovers sighed,
   And talked of the old time far away
  When the roses were red at La Garraye,
When the gay young lord and his fair young bride
Rode forth on their swift steeds, side by side,

And met the sudden and terrible blight —
   Like the lightning flash from a summer cloud
  Followed by thunder long and loud —
That turned, in an instant, their noon to night,
And slew, not Love, but Love's delight.

And they pitied those lovers of long ago —
   These modern lovers that told the tale —
  And honored the love that could not fail:
And she said, — "My dear, do you love *me* so?"
And he, — "Do you love *me*, and do not know?"

Then he gathered those blossoms of ruin and blight,
   And — "I give you the roses of Love," said he :
   "No, you give me the roses of Death," said she,
"The roses that spring from sorrow and night,
For love and for living too coldly white."

She shuddered a little, yet pinned them fast —
   The pallid roses of Fate were they,
   And died at the close of a brief bright day,
Like a brief bright love that came and passed,
Leaving only its ghost at last.

NOW AND THEN.

AND had you loved me then, my dear,
    And had you loved me there,
When still the sun was in the east
    And hope was in the air, —
When all the birds sang to the dawn
    And I but sang to you, —
Oh, had you loved me then, my dear,
    And had you then been true!

But ah! the day wore on, my dear,
    And when the noon grew hot
The drowsy birds forgot to sing,
    And you and I forgot
To talk of love, or live for faith,
    Or build ourselves a nest;
And now our hearts are shelterless,
    Our sun is in the west.

"THE KING IS DEAD, LONG LIVE THE KING."

Do you see how the Old Year hides his eyes,
    Hides his eyes as he steals away?
Yet they shone like stars with a glad surprise
    Only a twelvemonth ago to-day.
He had come to be king o'er the world of men;
    Gifts he had brought in his lavish hand,
And we, his subjects, trusted him then,
    And shouted and laughed at the king's command.

The bells they rang, and the people cheered,
    And the preachers praised him and welcomed him in —
Never a king more royal appeared,
    Or ever was hailed with a lordlier din.
Then, sooth, he began his gifts to bestow,
    As a monarch might on a waiting band
Of his courtiers, smiling and bowing below,
    Waiting his pleasure and kissing his hand.

He was a giver impartial as Fate, —
    Donor to one and donor to all, —
And the crowds that gathered his pleasure to wait
    Caught each of them something his hand let fall:

To these it was Love, that is strong as life ;
   To those it was Death, more tender than love ;
To some it was victory after strife,
   To others defeat and the sorrow thereof.

Till at last his courtiers grew ill content,
   And each man sighed for his neighbor's dole,
And the Year was old, and his strength was spent —
   Toll the bell for his parting soul !
Toll, but be glad, for the old should die,
   And love and life belong to the new —
Why over the Old Year should we sigh?
   He was but a niggard to me — to you.

But this glad New Year, with smiles in his eyes,
   This new young king, who is good to see,
He will make us happy and wealthy and wise,
   And for him we will clamor joyously —
Shout till our throats with shouting are hoarse,
   Ring the bells and kindle the fires,
For he will bring to us joy, perforce —
   Give to our hearts our hearts' desires.

Surely he cannot be stern or sad, —
   He, with the light in his shining eyes, —
We, his subjects, shall all be glad,
   Dowered at last with some sweet surprise :
What the hard Old Year to our prayers denied
   We shall win from the New Year, glad and gay,
And live, with his bounty satisfied, —
   Welcome him in ! It is New Year's Day.

Sonnets in Many Moods.

Scorn not the Sonnet.
                    WORDSWORTH.

It is the violoncello, or else man's heart's complaint.
                    WALT WHITMAN.

HELEN'S CUP.

GIVE me the potent draught that Helen poured
    To lull Telemachus! Make me forget
All present peril, all old sins, and let
Me dream, in peace. Long threat'ning, Fate's
    sharp sword
Before my eyes has hung — about me roared
   The battle's clamor. Sore I am beset —
   New fears and ancient pains together met
Assail me, who for peace have long implored:

Give me at last to drink, and let them flee,
The baffled ghosts that watch me sullenly,
   To those waste fields that waiting shadows keep;
   And down some waveless tide, in quiet deep
As set of day upon a quiet sea,
   Oh, let me drift and dream, and fall on sleep!

SILENT SORROW.

IF she unclosed her lips and made her moan
    She would not be so weary with her woe —
A burden shared is lightened: even so
The weight is heavier that we bear alone,
And anguish, pent within, turns hearts to stone.
    The fellowship of sorrow to forego —
    To suffer and be silent — is to know
The blackest blossom from the black root grown.

And yet great joys and greatest woes are dumb:
    Small is the sum that reckoning can compute —
    The shallows babble, but the depths are mute —
The great mid-sea our measure may not plumb:
King Love, King Pain, King Death, in silence come;
    And, meeting them, we silently salute.

A CRY.

O WANDERER in unknown lands, what cheer?
   How dost thou fare on thy mysterious way?
What strange light breaks upon thy distant day,
Yet leaves me lonely in the darkness here?
Oh, bide no longer in that far-off sphere:
   Though all Heaven's cohorts should thy footsteps stay,
   Break through their splendid, militant array,
And answer to my call, O dead and dear!

I shall not fear thee, howsoe'er thou come;
Thy coldness will not chill, though Death *is* cold;
   A touch, and I shall know thee, — or a breath;
Speak the old, well-known language, or be dumb;
Only come back! Be near me as of old;
   So thou and I shall triumph over Death!

LOVE'S EMPTY HOUSE.

O THOU long-silent, solitary house,
   Where Love once came and went with joyous
      cries,
Or lingered long, sighing as Summer sighs
When Autumn's breath begins her fear to rouse
With fierce caress that shall make bare her boughs,
   Her tender boughs, and all her beauty's prize
   Deliver, faded, to the winds that rise
And rend her crown from her dishonored brows! —

O solitary house! thine open door
   Again shall welcome sweet Love's wingèd tread;
His eyes shall light thee, as they lit of yore
   In days when Love and Joy were newly wed;
   He shall return with myrtle round his head,
And fill thy halls with music as before.

AFTER DEATH.

*And very sweet it is
To know he still is warm though I am cold.*
                               CHRISTINA ROSSETTI.

I WOULD not have thee warm when I am cold;
  But both together — 'neath some sylvan mound,
Amid the pleasant secrets under ground,
Where green things flourish in the embracing mould,
And jealous seeds the souls of blossoms hold —
  In some sweet fellowship of silence bound,
  Deeper than life, more exquisite than sound,
Rest tranquilly while Love's new tales are told.

We will not grudge the waking world its bliss,
  Its joy of speech, its gladness of surprise,
When lovers clasp each others hands and kiss
  And earth puts on new glory to their eyes:
  We, lying there with Death's deep knowledge wise,
Shall know that we have found Life's best in this

VOICES ON THE WIND.

FAR out at sea I hear the wind complain, —
    With the old plaint that vexed my childish ear,
  And seemed the cry of spirits drawing near
To sob their incommunicable pain.
Whence did they come, and whither go again?
    My very heart stood still with sudden fear
    When the forlorn approach I used to hear
Of all the shuddering, melancholy train.

And lo, in this night's vigil far at sea,
    The same long cry! — Are they unpardoned yet?
      Does the old pain still goad them till they come,
Unsheltered souls, to sob once more to me
    Of some dead wrong they never can forget
      Till there is no more sea, and winds are dumb?

THE CUP OF DEATH.

FOR A PICTURE BY ELIHU VEDDER.

SHE bends her lovely head to taste thy draught,
   O thou stern Angel of the Darker Cup!
With thee to-night in the dim shades to sup,
Where all they be who from that cup have quaffed.
She had been glad in her own loveliness, and laughed
   At Life's strong enemies who lie in wait;
   Had kept with golden youth her queenly state,
All unafraid of Sorrow's threat'ning shaft.

Then human Grief found out her human heart,
   And she was fain to go where pain is dumb;
     So Thou wert welcome, Angel dread to see,
     And she fares onward with thee, willingly,
To dwell where no man loves, no lovers part, —
   Thus Grief that is, makes welcome Death to come.

TO A MODERN POET.

WITH A COPY OF "SHAKSPEARE'S SONNETS."

TAKE thou these words thine elder brother writ, —
   Thou, to whom Song is as thy native speech !
Across the swift-flown centuries thou canst reach
To him, thy kinsman, reverent hands and sit —
While shadows of the Past about ye flit —
   With him, " in sessions of sweet, silent thought,"
   And share with him those halcyon days that brought
Music's sweet charm, and sparkle keen of wit.

So shalt thou learn the secret of his song, —
   Those minor chords ; since Life is as the leaf,
   And gladdest love and brightest day are brief ;
Those clear, bold notes that told his soul was strong,
Brave to endure, and swift to smite the wrong,
   Until Death healed thine elder brother's grief.

THE LAST GOOD-BY.

How shall we know it is the last good-by?
    The skies will not be darkened in that hour,
  No sudden blight will fall on leaf or flower,
No single bird will hush its careless cry,
And you will hold my hands, and smile or sigh
    Just as before. Perchance the sudden tears
    In your dear eyes will answer to my fears;
But there will come no voice of prophecy, —

No voice to whisper, "Now, and not again,
    Space for last words, last kisses, and last prayer,
For all the wild, unmitigated pain
    Of those who, parting, clasp hands with despair," —
"Who knows?" we say, but doubt and fear remain,
    Would any *choose* to part thus unaware?

LOVE IS DEAD.

I HEARD one cry out strongly, "Love is dead!"
    And then we went and looked upon his face,
  Turned into marble by Death's final grace:
His silent lips, that once so vainly pled,
Smile now, as men smile being newly wed;
    Since some strange joy Life's sorrows did efface
    When Death's arms clasped him in supreme embrace,
All his long pain of living comforted.

And you would wake him? Dare you him recall
    From Death's enamouring to Life's stern pain;
Make him again the old grief's hopeless thrall;
    Bind him once more with the old clanking chain,
    And goad him on his weary way again?—
Nay! let him rest with Death, the lord of all.

HIC JACET.

SO Love is dead that has been quick so long!
    Close, then, his eyes, and bear him to his rest,
  With eglantine and myrtle on his breast,
And leave him there, their pleasant scents among;
And chant a sweet and melancholy song
    About the charms whereof he was possessed,
    And how of all things he was loveliest,
And to compare with aught were him to wrong.

Leave him beneath the still and solemn stars,
    That gather and look down from their far place
      With their long calm our brief woes to deride,
Until the Sun the Morning's gate unbars
    And mocks, in turn, our sorrows with his face; —
      And yet, had Love been Love, he had not died.

LEFT BEHIND.

WILT thou forget me in that other sphere, —
   Thou who hast shared my life so long in this, —
And straight grown dizzy with that greater bliss,
Fronting heaven's splendor strong and full and clear,
No longer hold the old embraces dear
   When some sweet seraph crowns thee with her kiss?
   Nay, surely from that rapture thou wouldst miss
Some slight, small thing that thou hast cared for here.

I do not dream that from those ultimate heights
   Thou wilt come back to seek me where I bide;
But if I follow, patient of thy slights,
   And if I stand there, waiting by thy side,
Surely thy heart with some old thrill will stir,
And turn thy face toward me, even from her.

FUTURE FORGIVENESS.

How long wilt thou be silent, lying there?
   I grieved thee once, and now my heart makes moan,
  Cries, and thou wilt not answer, turned to stone,
And pitiless as stone to my despair:
My tears fall on thee, and thou dost not care:
   Oh! art thou cruel now who wast so kind;
   Or only to my sorrow deaf and blind —
Gone on beyond the hearing of my prayer?

Shall it not be that in thy brighter life
   I find thee, move thee to some pitying thrill,
    And win thee by my pleading to forgive?
Thou couldst forget past folly and past strife,
   Seeing, in that new sphere, I love thee still;
    And thou — didst thou not love thou wouldst not live.

IN PACE.

WHEN I am dead, with mockery of praise
    Thou shalt not vex the stillness of my sleep:
Leave me to long tranquillity and deep,
Who, through such weary nights and lonesome days,
Such hopeless stretch of uncompanioned ways,
    Have come at length my quiet rest to keep
    Where nettles thrive, and careless brambles creep,
And things that love the dark their dull brood raise.

After my restless years I would have rest, —
    Long rest after so many restless years, —
    Unmocked by hope, set free from haunting fears;
    Since some old pain might waken at thy tread,
Do thou for once in this my heart's behest,
    Come thou not nigh when I am lying dead.

A WOMAN'S KNOWLEDGE.

A ROSE to smell a moment, then to leave,
    Chance strain of song you smile at as you pass,
  Bubble that breaks before you lip the glass,
Chain frail as the frail thread that spiders weave;
Oh, do not think that I myself deceive!
    Thus, and not otherwise, to you am I, —
    A moment's pleasure as you pass me by,
Powerless, at best, to make you joy or grieve.

And you, to me, my sun-god and my sun,
    Who warmed my heart to life with careless ray!
    Forever will that burning memory stay
And warm me in the grave when life is done: —
What farther grace has any woman won?
    Since your chance gift you cannot take away.

IN SOLITUDE.

HAVE pity thou, who all my heart hast known!
  Come back from thy far place and heal my
    pain!
My long, unshared, uncheered days wax and wane;
The strong suns mock me, I am so alone;
The hurrying winds sweep by, nor heed my moan;
  The climbing stars of night, a shining train,
  With curious eyes behold me wait in vain, —
And Nature's very self doth me disown.

I did not know how blessed I was, God wot,
  When thy dear voice made music for my ears,
  Fostered my starveling joys and shamed my fears:
Now thou art dumb; and I, by thee forgot,
  Live through the empty, pitiless months and years
And think how I was glad, yet knew it not.

BEYOND SIGHT AND SOUND.

FULL soon I shall be gone, where dead men go, —
    Gone on, beyond your ken, far out of sight —
To that dim, phantom world that no stars light ;
Where souls like pallid flames flit to and fro,
Where Love is not, nor memory of Woe,
    And no voice pleads through that eternal night ;
    Dumb are those souls, and dead is their delight,
They need no courage, since no fear they know.

If a sad ghost should seem to bar your way,
    Think not from that vague world that I return ;
'T will be but moonlight silvering some spray.
    I shall not hear you, howso'er you yearn ;
Yet if your cry *could* follow my far track,
I think from bane or bliss I should come back.

TO ONE WHO HAS LOVED OFTEN.

PALIMPSEST heart, on which so many names
    Love's hand has writ! Blind Love, could he not know
    Which one was the true script of Fate, and thus forego
To lend his torch to kindle transient flames?
New risen joy each new day's sun proclaims;
    Each dawning sets the amorous east aglow;
    Each day is bright until its sun is low;
As of fair days, so is it of fair dames.

Why should we chide the glad who find life sweet?
    Their careless hearts are like a favored year,
    All blessed summer; or a garden ground
To which no frosts come, where no tempests beat,
    But roses bloom forever, red and dear,
    And blithe birds fill it always with sweet sound.

BEFORE THE SHRINE.

I BUILT a shrine, and set my idol there,
   And morn and noon and night my knees I bent,
   And cried aloud until my strength was spent,
Beseeching his cold pity with my prayer.
Sometimes at dawning, when the day was fair,
   A ray of light to his stern visage sent
   The semblance of a smile. "Does he relent,"
I cried, "this strong god, Love, whose high-priest is
    Despair?"

But noon came on, and in its full, clear light
   I saw his lips, as ruthless as of old;
   And his eyes mocked me like relentless fate,
Till I was fain to hide me from his sight;
   Then one swept off from him his mantle's fold,
   And lo, my idol was not Love, but Hate.

ROSES AT SEA.

LOVE-CHILDREN of the summer and the sun,
    Alien to this salt air and stretch of sea,
  And beautiful in your bright witchery
As the first rose, whose wooing was begun
By the first nightingale, when day was done
    And over Eden's walks the wind blew free,
    And the winged wooers sang in ecstasy
Of love and love and love — till love was won.

To-day you bless me with your beauty's spell,
    Roses from some dream-garden left behind,
With breath half tenderness and half farewell,
    And gracious hopes with your sweet grace entwined :
Will hopes, like buds, turn blossoms? Who shall tell?
    Your fragrant soul escapes — can Memory bind?

A GHOST'S QUESTION.

WHEN with your fair, new Love you laughing go
    Through the loud streets we two have known
       so well,
  Will not old memories your feet compel
To wait, sometimes, for one whose step is slow,
Whose presence only you may feel or know,—
    The shadow of a shadow, you dispel
    With wave of hand, as the old tale you tell
To new ears listening as I used, you know?

Or when you press her hand against your breast,
  Will you for one swift instant think it mine,
And thrill to the dead joy you once possessed
    And quaffed and savored, as men quaff their wine—
Then turn and meet her smile, jest back her jest,
  And swear afresh she doth all charms combine?

SISTER SORROW.

I FOUND her walking in a lonely place,
   Where shadows lingered and the day was low;
     She trod a devious path with footsteps slow,
And by the waning light I scanned her face,
And in its pensive loveliness beheld the trace
   Old tears had left, and woes of long ago;
     Then knew she I was kin to her, and so
Stretched forth her chill, soft hand with welcoming
   grace.

Now I walk with her through her realm of shade —
   I hear gay music sound, and laughter ring,
     And voices call me that I knew of old,
But of their mocking mirth I am afraid, —
   Led through the dusk by her to whom I cling,
     May I not reach some blessedness untold?

HE LOVED.

"HE loved me once!" What words are these —
    "He loved!"
  Past tense, past love, past joy, past hope, past
    dream, —
All things that were and are not, — how they seem
To crowd around and mock the love disproved,
The former bliss, by ages long removed;
  The light, far off as farthest star's pale beam
  That sheds through trackless space its fitful gleam,
Which once, our sun, we welcomed and approved.

How dear that was which lies here stark and dead
  While we sit watching in God's awful sight,
He knows; but hath no dew of healing shed,
  Nor any grace doth proffer us, — by night
And change and death who are discomfited, —
  No single hope to turn our dark to light.

HEREAFTER.

IN after years a twilight ghost shall fill
    With shadowy presence all thy waiting room :
  From lips of air thou canst not kiss the bloom ;
Yet at old kisses will thy pulses thrill,
And the old longing, that thou couldst not kill,
    Feeling her presence in the gathering gloom,
    Will mock thee with the hopelessness of doom,
While she stands there and smiles, serene and still.

Thou canst not vex her, then, with passion's pain :
    Call, and the silence will thy call repeat ;
    But she will smile there, with cold lips and sweet,
Forgetful of old tortures, and the chain
That once she wore, the tears she wept in vain
    At passing from her threshold of thy feet.

AT WAR.

THROUGH the large, stormy splendors of the night,
  When clouds made war, and spears of moonlight strove
  To penetrate their serried ranks and prove
That braver than the darkness was the light,
Yet failed before the storm-clouds' gathered might,
  I heard a voice cry, "Strong indeed is Love,
  But stronger Fate and Death, who hold above
Their pitiless, high court, in Love's despite."

Storm-cloud met storm-cloud, reeled, and shook, and fled, —
  The old earth trembled at their mighty rage, —
Till, suddenly, a lark sang clear o'erhead,
  As if to share his joy he did engage
All earth and heaven; and Night's wild war was done,
And Love and Morning triumphed with the sun.

NEAR, YET FAR.

SO near! and yet, I think, as far apart
    As heaven from hell, high noon from darkest
       night,
Or buried face, from longing lover's sight:
I dream of you, and then from dreams I start
To hear the beating of my own sad heart,
    That snatched from dreams impossible delight,
    But quickly wakes again, in wretched plight,
To meet the day's keen pain and ceaseless smart.

How shall I comfort, then, my lonesome years —
    Since dreams are dim, and sleeping time is brief — ?
For very full I am of restless fears,
    Blown to and fro, as is a vagrant leaf;
And well I know how idle are the tears
    That burn my aching eyes, yet mock my grief.

A FALLEN HOUSE.

THE end has come, which never seems the end;
    And thou and I, who loved so long and well,
  Find at the last our Fate implacable, —
Stern Fate, who wills not that our lives shall blend,
And overthrows fair things we did intend.
    The house in which long time we thought to dwell,
  Was built above a ruin — so it fell.
Great was the fall, which no man could defend.

Behold it lies there overthrown, that house!
In its fair halls no comer shall carouse;
  Its broad rooms with strange silences are filled;
No fire upon its crumbling hearth shall glow —
Seeing its desolation, men shall know
  On ruin of what was they may not build.

MY MOURNER.

I LIE here very still; and he draws nigh
   To stand beside me, and to look his last
On her who far beyond his ken has passed,
Yet rests here, 'neath his touch, so tranquilly;
From the shut lips there comes no least, low sigh;
   No eyelash quivers, and white Death holds fast,
   In long embrace by longing dreams forecast,
The life that had known Life's satiety.

I laughed and loved and wept, and now I sleep;
   And that were best of all, if no dreams come
To mar this quietude of slumber, deep
     And still as some deep night when winds are dumb;
But he, my mourner, wherefore should he keep
   Intrusive vigil round my silent home?

AT SEA.

OUTSIDE the mad sea ravens for its prey,
   Shut from it by a floating plank I lie;
  Through this round window search the faithless sky,
The hungry waves that fain would rend and slay,
The live-long, blank, interminable way,
   Blind with the sun and hoarse with the wind's cry
   Of wild, unconquerable mutiny,
Until night comes more terrible than day.

No more at rest am I than wind and wave;
   My soul cries with them in their wild despair,
I, who am Destiny's impatient slave,
   Who find no help in hope, nor ease in prayer,
And only dream of rest, on some dim shore
Where sea and storm and life shall be no more.

LAURA SLEEPING.

COME hither and behold this lady's face,
  Who lies asleep, as if strong Death had kissed
  Upon her eyes the kiss none can resist,
And held her fast in his prolonged embrace!
See the still lips, which grant no answering grace
  To Love's fond prayers, and the sweet, carven smile,
  Sign of some dream-born joy which did beguile
The dreaming soul from its fair resting-place!

So will she look when Death indeed has sway
  O'er her dear loveliness, and holds her fast
In that last sleep which knows nor night, nor day,
  Which hopes no future, contemplates no past;
So *will* she look; but now, behold! she wakes —
Thus, from the Night, Dawn's sunlit beauty breaks.

TO ONE MOST UNHAPPY.

IF I should see thee, Most Unhappy, dead,
   How should I dare to utter moan for thee?
 Does any grieve for prisoner set free?
Or shall our tears upon his brow be shed
Who after long starvation full is fed?
   Nay, rather, clamor, bells, exultantly;
   Like wedding chimes ring out your harmony;
Since saddest Life to gladdest Death is wed.

Thou, whose whole life was sorrow! In thy grave
   Shall not strange joy possess thee, and deep rest;
     Such rest as no man knoweth, having breath?
Wilt thou not hear from far the old blasts rave
   That long pursued thee with relentless quest,
     And know them mocked, at last, by thee and
       Death?

IN THE COURT OF THE LIONS:

BY MOONLIGHT.

THESE lions were sculptured centuries ago
    In that fair court a Sultan made for her
Who was his heart's delight.   Her worshipper
Was he whom all men worshipped; proving so
His love and homage that the ages know
    How fair she was, and how at softest stir
    Of her soft robes — as these proud courts aver —
His kingly heart with kingly love did glow;

Till he bade crafty workmen come and make
A palace, lovely for her lovely sake,
    Thick-set with gems, with many a sculptured space
Wrought cunningly out of the creamy stone
    To frame the dusky beauty of her face, —
Still on those courts the white moon shines, but *they*
      are gone!

ALHAMBRA, SPAIN, 1883.

MY CASTLE.

A SPANISH Castle long ago I built,
   Where Love and I might keep our holiday;
In its fair court the fountain's sparkling play
Plashed light and music, and the happy lilt
Of singing birds with yellow sunshine gilt
   Called — mate to mate — in amorous roundelay;
   And there, I thought, sweet Love might live alway,
And my libation to the gods I spilt.

Fair 'gainst the western sky my Castle rose;
   Men envied me who saw its turrets shine
     Agleam with sunset lights of burning gold;
And Love was lord, and well to rule Love knows,
   And I was his, and he was all divine —
     But I forgot that Love, himself, grows old.

BY MARCH WIND LED.

THE wild, beleaguering March wind storms my door,
  And in his wake surges an army vast, —
  Old Hopes, old Dreams, old Love, too dear to last,
And all that made life glad in days of yore,
Turned now to ghosts, and from their alien shore
  Come back for this one night to bring my Past,
  And vex me with its spell about me cast,
Though It and I be parted evermore.

Beleaguering host! I bid ye now avaunt!
  I will not listen, though ye call for aye.
  As pitiless as blasts from this March sky
I found ye once. What right have ye to haunt
  This night that should be peaceful? I defy
Your evil power — my soul ye shall not daunt.

MY MOTHER'S PICTURE.

How shall I here her placid picture paint
    With touch that shall be delicate, yet sure?
  Soft hair above a brow so high and pure
Years have not soiled it with an earthly taint,
Needing no aureole to prove her saint;
    Firm mind that no temptation could allure;
    Soul strong to do, heart stronger to endure;
And calm, sweet lips that utter no complaint.

So have I seen her, in my darkest days
    And when her own most sacred ties were riven,
Walk tranquilly in self-denying ways,
    Asking for strength, and sure it would be given;
Filling her life with lowly prayer, high praise, —
    So shall I see her, if we meet in heaven.

AT A RUINED ABBEY.

THE gray day's ending followed the gray day,—
   All gray together, ruin and air and sky,—
  And a lone wind of memory whispered by,
And told dark secrets on its wandering way;
Through the blank windows' space, like ghosts astray,
   Sad crowds of black-winged jackdaws came and
     went—
  Were they dead monks on some strange penance
    sent,
Who used within these walls to preach and pray?

Do they return, from the far, starry sphere,
   To their old haunt within these ruins old,
     To celebrate, perchance, some mystic rite,
Some yearning soul's outcry of pain to hear;
   And, when the awful story has been told,
     Will priest and sinner vanish on the night?

His Second Wife Speaks.

— · —

If two lives join there is oft a scar,
They are one and one with a shadowy third.

BROWNING.

I.

A PARABLE.

I LONGED for rest and, some one spoke me fair,
    And proffered goodly rooms wherein to dwell,
  Hung round with tapestries, and garnished well,
That I might take mine ease and pleasure there;
And there I sought a refuge from despair,
    A joy that should my life's long gloom dispel;
    But ominously through those halls there fell
Strange sounds, as of old music in the air.

As day went down, the music grew apace,
    And in the moonlight saw I, white and cold,
A presence radiant in the radiant space,
    With smiling lips that never had grown old;
    And then I knew the secret none had told,
And shivered there, an alien in that place.

II.

SILENT.

I WILL not speak. For ever from old days
    Another voice assails him; shall mine come
  To break that perfect music? Make me dumb,
God, who art merciful! and of thy grace
Keep my lips silent. I have heard him praise
    Her speech, as sweet as late bird singing home,
    And soft as on far shore breaks the pale foam,
Tender as twilight's peace on woodland ways.

I serve his pleasure, wait with ears attent;
    Indeed, it well befits me to be meek:
His joy is passed, his fortune has been spent,
    And I — he found me when he turned to seek,
In place of bliss, some pale and dull content —
    I will be faithful, but I will not speak.

III.

A SECOND PLACE.

I WOULD, indeed, that Heaven had made me meek,
   Content to hold and fill a second place,
   Take lesser love as undeservèd grace,
And bow my thankful head when one should speak
Me gently, touch with careless hand my cheek,
   Or bend sometimes and kiss my unpraised face,
   Since she, forsooth, is in her far-off place
For whom his highest homage seemed too weak.

But I was made with passionate, strong soul,
   And what I would, I would have wholly mine;
And if I bow my head to Love's control,
   And to his keeping all myself consign,
It must be Love that answers to my need,
That loves me wholly, and is Love indeed.

IV.

ALONE IN DEATH.

ALONE in Death I think my heart will be;
    I have no dead to wait me in that land,
  And if with thee I entered, hand in hand,
When her voice called wouldst thou not turn from
      me,
And leave me lonely by that jasper sea —
    Lonely, forever, on that silent strand,
    When with entreaty stronger than command
Her languorous, low tones invited thee?

And she would find my kisses on thy mouth,
    And yet forgive thee with a royal grace,
Because, when she had gone, too long the drouth,
    The uncheered waiting her divine embrace —
And I, O God! should long to die again,
Yet face my immortality of pain.

V.

FACE TO FACE.

THOU gazest in mine eyes and thine are wet;
    Thy hand seeks mine, and clings, and holds
        me fast;
"The present," dost thou say, "and not the past
Means light and joy and hope. I am beset
With idle fears. Thy heart in my heart met
    Its all of love and faith — the spell I cast
    Will bind thee, while the soul in thee shall last,
And the next life shall pay this life's dear debt."

Thine eyes seem true! Thy words! Ah *she* can
    hear!
    From her high place I think she sees thee now;
Draw back thine hand, if but one shade of fear
    Of her reproach assail thee. I will bow
To Fate's decree — from blame thou shalt be clear —
    Thou wilt not? . . . We will face her, — I and
        thou!

The Still Hour.

The holy time is quiet as a nun,
Breathless with adoration.
                    WORDSWORTH.

IN THE PINE WOODS AT MARIENBAD.

DEDICATED TO LOUISA, LADY ASHBURTON.

HERE come we, to this temple strange and vast;
   Here is the shadowy stillness meet for prayer,
And here such fragrance breathes upon the air
That it must be Heaven's own high-priests have passed
And to the winds a heavenly incense cast;
   Far up against the blue we see them there,
   Glad messengers, that on God's errands fare —
Oh may we join their shining ranks at last!

This is the noblest Church was ever reared!
   Shall we not enter here to praise and pray,
     To kneel within its mighty nave and cry
To Him, our God, beloved of us and feared,
   Whose light must guide us on our devious way,
     Whose help must reach us, or we helpless die?

AT MARIENBAD, September, 1887.

HELP THOU MY UNBELIEF!

BECAUSE I seek thee not, oh seek Thou me!
    Because my lips are dumb, oh hear the cry
  I do not utter as Thou passest by,
And from my life-long bondage set me free!
Because content I perish, far from Thee,
    Oh seize me, snatch me from my fate, and try
    My soul in Thy consuming fire! Draw nigh
And let me, blinded, Thy salvation see.

If I were pouring at Thy feet my tears,
    If I were clamoring to see Thy face,
        I should not need Thee, Lord, as now I need,
Whose dumb, dead soul knows neither hopes nor
        fears,
    Nor dreads the outer darkness of this place —
        Because I seek not, pray not, give Thou heed!

SHALL I LOOK BACK?

FROM some dim height of being, undescried,
    Shall I look back and trace the weary way
  By which my feet are journeying to-day, —
The toilsome path that climbs the mountain-side
Or leads into the valley, sun-denied,
    Where, through the darkness, hapless wanderers
        stray,
  Unblessed, uncheered, ungladdened by a ray
Of certitude their errant steps to guide?

Shall I look back, and see the great things small;
    The toilsome path, God's training for my feet,
      The pains that never had been worth my tears?
Will some great light of rapture, bathing all,
    Make by-gone woe seem joy; past bitter, sweet?
      Shall I look back and wonder at my fears?

STRAIGHT ON TO PORT.

STRAIGHT through the sea-foam and the awful sea,
  And winds that battle round us day and night,
  Till the pale moon hides her white face in fright,
The ship that bears my longing heart and me
Fares toward that port where waiting loved ones be,
  And on the hearth of home the fire is bright;
  There wistful eyes shall be made glad with sight,
And perils past forgotten joyfully.

So, through long nights, and brief, sad winter days,
  Or summer's short-lived triumphs, or young springs,
Or autumn's wind-blown, melancholy ways,
  My soul bears onward to her haven far,
  Beyond the utmost sea's dim harbor-bar,
There to forget what storms have bruised her wings.

    AT SEA, 1884.

A PRAYER IN SORROW.

MY heart is at Thy feet, — my helpless heart!
    I pray Thee bend and listen to my prayer;
Bend low, and comfort my most deep despair,
Since my sole help, sole comforter Thou art.
It is thy will that Joy and I should part;
    Thy will be done — but have me in Thy care;
    Unhelped by Thee the load I cannot bear —
My heart is at Thy feet, my helpless heart.

How can I go alone through life to death,
    Confront each empty day and lonely night,
Each doubt and fear my soul that challengeth,
    Except Thy strong arm put my foes to flight?
I cry to Thee, who gave my spirit breath —
    Save me — O strong to save, as strong to smite!

ON HOMEWARD WING.

FROM the soft south the constant bird comes back,
    Faith-led, to find the welcome of the spring
In the old boughs whereto she used to cling
Before she sought the unknown southward track:
Above the Winter and the storm-cloud's wrack
    She hears the prophecy of days that bring
    The Summer's pride, and plumes her homeward
        wing
To seek again the joys that exiles lack.

Shall I of little faith, less brave than she,
    Set forth unwillingly my goal to find,
    Go home from exile with reluctant mind,
Distrust the steadfast stars I cannot see,
    And doubt the heavens because my eyes are blind?
Nay! Give me faith like wings to soar to Thee!

IN MID-OCEAN.

ACROSS this sea I sail, and do not know
    What hap awaits me on its farther side, —
  In these long days what dear hope may have died;
What sweet, accustomed joy I must forego;
What new acquaintance make with unguessed woe
    (I, who with sorrow have been long allied,)
  Or what blest gleam of joy yet undescried
Its tender light upon my way will throw.

Thus over Death's unsounded sea we sail,
    Toward a far, unmapped, unpictured shore,
Unwitting what awaits us, bliss or bale,
    Like the vast multitude that went before,
Scourged on by the inexorable gale
    The everlasting mystery to explore.

    AT SEA, 1888.

AS IN VISION.

SOMETIMES in heaven-sent dreams I do behold
    A city with its turrets high in air,
  Its gates that gleam with jewels strange and rare,
And streets that glow with burning of red gold;
And happy souls, through blessedness grown bold,
    Thrill with their praises all the radiant air,
  And God himself is light, and shineth there
On glories tongue of man hath never told.

And in my dreams I thither march, nor stay
    To heed earth's voices, howso'er they call,
Or proffers of the joys of this brief day,
    On which so soon the sunset shadows fall;
I see the gleaming gates, and toward them press —
What though my path lead through the wilderness?

A PRAYER FOR LIGHT.

I KNEEL before Thee, Lord, oh hear my cry;
   From its sore burden set my spirit free,
And give my longing wings to soar toward Thee
Through the pure ether of the upper sky,
And find Thee, *find Thee*, though Thou art so high!
   Give me to eat from that most sacred tree
   Whose leaves of healing wave eternally —
Fed full of life by Thee, I shall not die,

Or, dying, die but to be newly born
   In that glad day whereof Thou art the light, —
The light whose glories do eclipse the morn,
   And blind the sun, and put to death the night —
O Life, O Light, O God, let me be Thine;
Sun of all worlds, upon my darkness shine!

COME UNTO ME.

I HEAR the low voice call that bids me come, —
   Me, even me, with all my grief oppressed,
  With sins that burden my unquiet breast,
And in my heart the longing that is dumb,
Yet beats forever, like a muffled drum,
   For all delights whereof I, dispossessed,
   Pine and repine, and find nor peace nor rest
This side the haven where He bids me come.

He bids me come, and lay my sorrows down,
   And have my sins washed white by His dear grace;
He smiles — what matter, then, though all men frown?
   Naught can assail me, held in His embrace;
And if His welcome home the end may crown,
   Shall I not hasten to that heavenly place?

A RAINY AFTERNOON:

AT RAGATZ.

Dark are the clouds that hide from longing eyes
   The hills that glowed this morning with delight,
When the sun kindled height on shining height,
Pouring his splendor through the eastern skies.
From this dense gloom no Mounts of Visions rise, —
   The day forgets the magic of the morn, —
   Triumphant Darkness clothes itself with scorn,
And all Hope's auguries Despair defies.

Yet once again the sun shall gild the day,
   And once again the sun-kissed hills be glad,
And the vexed Earth go on its ancient way
   With all the old exultant joy it had;
And thou, faint heart, shall Darkness thee affright
While He still reigns who said, "Let there be light"?

   Ragatz, September, 1883.

HARK, TEN THOUSAND HARPS AND VOICES!

OH, strong and sweet these tones that seek the sky!
  Oh, sweet and strong the praises that I hear!
  When all hearts thrill, as one, with love and fear,
And all these voices, as with one voice, cry;
And Fear says, "Tremble, for God's throne is high;"
  And Love says, "Trust, because His heart is near,
  And all ye children to His heart are dear,
And God is love, and shall in love reply."

And then the music soars, as if on wings,
  And echoes fond the ecstasy prolong,
  Till waiting choirs of angels catch the song,
    And they in heaven and we on earth unite
    To sing His praise, and glorify His might,
Till unto God who hears His whole world sings.

Rosemary.

There's rosemary, — that's for remembrance.
SHAKSPEARE.

Into the night go one and all.
WILLIAM ERNEST HENLEY.

RALPH WALDO EMERSON.

HIS soul was one with Nature everywhere;
    Her seer and prophet and interpreter,
He waited in her courts for love of her,
And told the secrets that he gathered there,—
What flight the wild birds dared; why flowers were
    fair;
    The sense of that divine, tumultuous stir
    When Spring awakes, and all sweet things confer,
And youth and hope and joy are in the air.

Do the winds miss him, and the fields he knew,
    And the far stars that watched him night by night,
Looking from out their steadfast dome of blue
    To lead him onward with their tranquil light;
Or do they know what gates he wandered through,
    What heavenly glories opened on his sight?

AN OPEN DOOR.

City, of thine a single, simple door,
By some new Power reduplicate must be
Even yet my life-porch in eternity.
    DANTE GABRIEL ROSSETTI.

THAT longed-for door stood open, and he passed
  On through the star-sown fields of light, and stayed
Before its threshold, glad and unafraid,
Since all that Life or Death could do at last
Was over, and the hour so long forecast
  Had brought his footsteps thither. Undismayed
  He entered. Were his lips on her lips laid?
God knows. They met, and their new day was vast:

Night shall not darken it, nor parting blight:
  "Whatever is to know," they know it now:
  He comes to her with laurel on his brow,
Hero and conqueror from his life's fierce fight,
And Longing is extinguished in Delight, —
  "I still am I," his eyes say, "Thou art thou!"

BEHIND THE MIST:

IN THE ROOM WITH GEORGE FULLER'S PICTURES.

HE sent them forth, these softly gleaming shapes,
    And said, "Go, ye, and tread enchanted ground;
With veiling mists your paths I will surround,
And shield you from the careless crowd that gapes
On what all men can see. Your charm escapes
    Such gaze; by faithful lovers to be found
    Behind this tender veil that wraps you round,
And all your soft beguiling gently drapes."

And these fair people, whom his hand had made,
    And touched with sudden beauty, strange and sweet
    As the young Morn by the first Sun-ray kissed,
Live here, immortally and unafraid,
    While he — who can pursue his journeying feet?
    He has gone on, and up, behind the Mist.

HER GHOST.

IN MEMORY OF CICELEY NARNEY MARSTON.

I.

HER gentle ghost is with me everywhere!
   'Twas here she came, one summer day, to die;
Whispered my name, and then, all silently,
Laid her loved head upon the pillow there
And spoke no more. That summer day was fair
   And very glad with joyous minstrelsy
   Of choiring birds, and heedless gayety
Of small, bright things who of the sun were 'ware:

But, in the midmost glow of life, on Death
   She sudden chanced: he closed her dear, dark eyes;
The air grew heavy with her parting breath,
   And Nature seemed to shiver in surprise;
And then the things that morning had begun
Fared on — she too, like them, had sought the sun.

II.

NOW with the summer she has come again:
    Outside the birds sing as they sang that day,
And summer things upon the air are gay;
But she sits speechless, and her eyes are fain
To hide from me their mystery of pain. . . .
    From heaven to earth, oh, dim and far the way!
    Why hast thou come? Be merciful and say —
Of what strange wrong do thy veiled looks complain?

Hast thou brought back sad secrets from the skies;
    Or is it that the old days haunt thee still?
Is that immortal sorrow in thine eyes
    Token of longings Heaven could not fulfil?
Dear ghost, I pray thee answer, and forego
The stern resolve of thy unspoken woe.

III.

THOU wilt not speak! Day after silent day
    Thou sittest with me in this lonesome place:
The morning sunlight falls upon thy face;
Night comes, and thou and Night together stay,—
No sunshine warms thee, and no storms dismay.
    I stretch my empty arms for thine embrace
    Thou glidest from them with elusive grace:
Thine unresponsive lips will never say

The thing I long to hear; yet do I think,
    From me to thee, the living to the dead,
Waiting together on the hither brink
    Of Death's great middle sea, some influence shed
Must make thee know how now I hold thee dear,
Who loved thee not enough that other year.

AT END OF PAIN.

TO PHILLIP BOURKE MARSTON.

THY darkened life is over. Thou hast found
    That sweet, deep rest, which, through such
        lonesome days,
    And nights when sleep forsook thee, thou didst
        praise
With envious longing. In Death's silence drowned,
No clamoring bells with their intrusive sound,
    No noise of traffic in the city's maze,
    Or hurrying footsteps through its stony ways,
Will vex the slumber in which thou art bound.

Tired head, tired heart, tired spirit, all at rest ;
    Since for the weary rest is Death's first boon, —
        Rest ; and then, after rest, the waking joy ;
The sudden rapture, by new life possessed ;
    The swift, sure glory of the Heaven's high noon :
        The long-lost mother's welcome to her boy !

A SILENT GUEST.

TO H. E. C.

WE sit and chat in the familiar place, —
  We two, where in those other years were
      three, —
Till, suddenly, you turn your eyes from me,
And in the empty air I see a face,
Serenely smiling with the old-time grace,
  And we are three again. All silently
  The third guest entered; and as silent we,
Held mute by very awe for some brief space.

And then we question — Has he come to stay?
  Was heaven lonely to the child of earth?
    Was there no nectar in immortal bliss
    For lips that thirsted for a mortal kiss?
  Has the new lesson taught the old love's worth?
The still ghost hears, and smiles, and — goes his way.

LOUISA M. ALCOTT.

IN MEMORIAM.

As the wind at play with a spark
   Of fire that glows through the night;
As the speed of the soaring lark
   That wings to the sky his flight;
So swiftly thy soul has sped
   On its upward, wonderful way,
Like the lark, when the dawn is red,
   In search of the shining day.

Thou art not with the frozen dead
   Whom earth in the earth we lay,
While the bearers softly tread,
   And the mourners kneel and pray;
From thy semblance, dumb and stark,
   The soul has taken its flight —
Out of the finite dark,
   Into the Infinite Light.

French Tunes.

Friend, let us pay the wonted fee.
>   ANDREW LANG.

Then let me live one long romance
   And learn to trifle well,
And write my motto " Vive la France!"
   And " Vive la bagatelle!"
>   WILLIAM MACKWORTH PRAED.

THE SPRING IS HERE.

I MISS you, sweet! The spring is here;
    The young grass trembles on the leas;
The violet's breath enchants the breeze;
And the blue sky bends low and near.

Home-coming birds, with carol clear,
    Make their new nests in budding trees —
I miss you, sweet, now spring is here
    And young grass trembles on the leas.

You were my Spring, and spring is dear;
    Without you can the May-time please?
    Let lavish June withhold her fees,
And winter reign throughout the year —
I miss you, sweet, though spring is here.

EASTER SUNDAY.

ON Easter morn she kneels and prays,
   A gentle saint in baby blue—
   Forgive her that her hat is new,
And all those dear, coquettish ways.

Her loyal soul pure tribute pays
   To that high throne where prayers are due,
At Easter, when she kneels and prays,
   A gentle saint in baby blue.

So innocent her girlish days
   She scarcely knows what sins to rue,
   What pard'ning grace from Heaven to sue,
As, glad with morning's gladdest rays,
A gentle saint, she kneels and prays.

HEART, SAD HEART.

HEART, sad heart, for what are you pleading?
   The sun has set, and the night is cold;
  To go on hoping were over bold;
Dead is the fire for want of feeding.

Tears are keeping your eyes from reading
   The old, old story, so often told —
Heart, sad heart, for what are you pleading?
   The sun has set, and the night is cold.

The wind and the rain in the dark are breeding
   Storms to sweep over valley and wold;
  Love, the outcast, with longing bold,
Clamors and prays to a power unheeding.
Heart, sad heart, for what are you pleading?

TWO RED ROSES.

TO M. R. L.

I WISH they could live forever, —
   These roses my darling brought !
  Their breath from her lips they caught,
And still with her touch they quiver.

As bright as their bright sweet giver,
   With a charm like her own charm fraught,
I wish they could live forever, —
   These roses my darling brought !

But loving from loved must sever,
   And hoping must come to nought —
  I know what the years have taught ;
Yet I wish they could live forever, —
   These roses my darling brought.

THE SHADOW DANCE.

SHE sees her image in the glass, —
   How fair a thing to gaze upon !
She lingers while the moments run,
With happy thoughts that come and pass,

Like winds across the meadow grass
   When the young June is just begun :
She sees her image in the glass, —
   How fair a thing to gaze upon !

What wealth of gold the skies amass !
   How glad are all things 'neath the sun !
   How true the love her love has won !
She recks not that this hour will pass ;
She sees her image in the glass.

IN FEBRUARY.

*And the second month of the year
   Puts heart in the earth again.*
                              P. B. MARSTON.

ALREADY the feet of the Winter fly,
   And the pulse of the Earth begins to leap,
Waking up from her frozen sleep,
And knowing the beautiful Spring is nigh.

Good Saint Valentine wanders by,
   Pausing his festival gay to keep;
Already the feet of the Winter fly,
   And the pulse of the Earth begins to leap.

To life she wakes; and a smile and a sigh —
   Language the scoffer holds so cheap —
   Thrill her with melody dear and deep.
Spring, with its mating time is nigh;
Already the feet of the Winter fly,
   And the pulse of the Earth begins to leap.

THE OLD BEAU.

HE was a gay deceiver when
    The century was young, they say,
And triumphed over other men,
    And wooed the girls, and had his way.

No maiden ever said him nay;
    No rival ever crossed him then;
    And painters vied to paint him when
The century was young, they say.

Now the new dogs must have their day;
    And the old beau has found that when
He pleads things go another way,
    And lonely 'mong the younger men,
    He hears their heartless laughter when
He boasts about that other day.

TO JOHN GREENLEAF WHITTIER,

ON HIS EIGHTIETH BIRTHDAY.

POET and friend, beloved of us so long,
  What shall we wish thee on thy natal day?
What rhymes and roses strew along thy way, —
Thine, unto whom all suffrages belong?

Through the dark night we caught thy thrilling song,
  Singer and prophet of the higher way:
Poet and friend beloved of us so long,
  What shall we wish thee on thy natal day?

Through all thy life the foe of every wrong,
  Strong of heart to labor, high of soul to pray,
  Guide to recall when errant footsteps stray;
What blessed memories round thy dear name throng!
Poet and friend, beloved of us so long,
  God bless and keep thee on thy natal day!

"WITH THOSE CLEAR EYES."

TO A. C. W.

LOOK at me, love, with those clear eyes
    In which I see the thoughts arise,
  As, gazing in a limpid well,
  Unto Narcissus it befell
To see himself with glad surprise.

Blue with the blue of summer skies, —
Dear skies, behind which heaven lies, —
  With one swift gaze my gloom dispel.
      Look at me, love!

See all my heart! Its weakest cries,
Its lonely prayers, its longing sighs,
  A language are which you can spell;
  You do not need what words can tell
On printed page to make you wise.
      Look at me, love!

LOVE'S GHOST.

IS Love at end?   How did he go?
   His coming was full sweet, I know;
  But when he went he slipped away
  And never paused to say good-day —
How could the traitor leave me so?

There's something in the summer, though,
That brings the old time back, and lo!
  This phantom that would bar my way
      Is dead Love's ghost.

His footfall is as soft as snow,
And in his path the lilies blow;
  He quenches the just-kindled ray
  With which I fain would light my way,
And bids me newer joys forego,
      This tyrant ghost.

HOW COULD I TELL?

HOW could I tell skies would be gray
    When you, dear heart, had gone away?
  How could I know the summer sun
  Was glad of you to look upon,
And it was you who warmed the day?

What part you had to make the May,
And how the very June was gay
  With something from your presence won,
    How could I tell?

When you were here, a fervid ray
Of sudden summer lit my way;
  Now you with love and life are done,
  The very light seems me to shun,
And through the dark I darkly stray —
    How could I tell?

WHEN LOVE WAS YOUNG.

WHEN Love was young, in days of yore,
    On bended knee full oft I swore
To him alone I 'd homage pay;
I 'd love forever and a day,
And love with every day the more.

I sang his praises o'er and o'er;
I conned no missal but his lore —
    Oh, but the world and I were gay
        When Love was young!

His blazonry the morning bore,
And all the larks that sing and soar
    Praised him upon their skyward way.
    . . . Ah, happy choir of yesterday,
        When Love was young!

IF LOVE COULD LAST.

IF Love could last, I'd spend my all
    And think the price was yet too small
  To buy his light upon my way,
  His sun to turn my night to day,
His cheer whatever might befall.

Were I his slave, or he my thrall,
No terrors should my heart appall;
    I'd fear no wreckage or dismay
        If Love could last.

Heaven's lilies grow up white and tall,
But warm within earth's garden wall
    With roses red the soft winds play —
    Ah, might I gather them to-day!
My hands should never let them fall,
        If Love *could* last.

O SWEETEST MAID!

TO M. R. L.

O SWEETEST maid, in other days
   The troubadours had sung your praise,
And knights had died and joyed to die
To win a smile as you passed by,
While lord and lackey stood at gaze.

What wonder that the task dismays
To wreathe your brow with modern bays,
   Or rhyming tricks for you to try,
      O sweetest maid!

For you should be those loftier lays
Of which from far the echo strays,
   In matchless, murmurous melody
   That dies in Love's divinest sigh —
Still Love's strong will my rhyme obeys,
      O sweetest maid!

IF YOU WERE HERE.

TO F. M. S.

IF you were here, or I were there,
   Then would I find the season fair.
  How blissfully the day would rise!
  How blue would be the summer skies!
And all the world a smile would wear.

What pleasant things we two would share!
By what green paths we two would fare!
  How sweet would be each day's surprise
     If you were here!

But now my joy is otherwhere;
Each day's a burden that I bear;
  And Pleasure mocks at me and flies,
  And Pain stands by my side and sighs;
And yet I know skies would be fair
     If you were here.

SUCH JOY IT WAS.

SUCH joy it was with Love to walk!
    The month it was the month of May
When we with Love began to talk.
Such joy it was with Love to walk
We did not see Fate's shadow stalk
    Beside us, where flowers hid the way,
Such joy it was with Love to walk —
    The month it was the month of May.

WE LOVED SO WELL.

WE loved so well in that old time;
　　But we and Love grew old together:
Old age forgets youth's golden prime.
We loved so well in that old time;
But youth and truth it is that rhyme,
　　And winter follows summer weather.
We loved so well in that old time;
　　But we and Love grew old together.

SO BLITHELY ROSE.

So blithely rose the happy day
    When you and I began to kiss,
The birds believed December May,
So blithely rose the happy day,
And blossoms bloomed along our way,
    Though it was time for snow, I wis, —
So blithely rose the happy day
    When you and I began to kiss.

THISTLE-DOWN.

THISTLE-DOWN is a woman's love, —
    Thistle-down with the wind at play.
Let him who wills this truth to prove,
" Thistle-down is a woman's love,"
Seek her innermost heart to move.
    Though the wind should blow her vows his way,
Thistle-down is a woman's love, —
    Thistle-down with the wind at play.

LOVE PLUMES HIS WINGS.

LOVE plumes his wings to fly away,
    And laughs to scorn our idle pain:
Ah, vain it is to laugh and pray!
Love plumes his wings to fly away:
What prayer of ours his flight can stay
    When, mocking us with high disdain,
Love plumes his wings to fly away,
    And laughs to scorn our idle pain?

IN WINTER.

OH, to go back to the days of June,
    Just to be young and alive again,
Hearken again to the mad sweet tune
    Birds were singing with might and main!
South they flew at the summer's wane,
    Leaving their nests for storms to harry,
Since time was coming for wind and rain
    Under the wintry skies to marry.

Wearily wander by dale and dune
    Footsteps fettered with clanking chain :
Free they were in the days of June ;
    Free they never can be again.
Fetters of age and fetters of pain,
    Joys that fly, and sorrows that tarry ;
Youth is over, and hope were vain
    Under the wintry skies to marry.

Now we chant but a desolate rune, —
    "Oh, to be young and alive again !"
But never December turns to June,
    And length of living is length of pain.

Winds in the nestless trees complain ;
    Snows of winter about us tarry ;
And never the birds come back again
    Under the wintry skies to marry.

ENVOI.

Youths and maidens, blithesome and vain,
    Time makes thrusts that you cannot parry ;
Mate in season, for who is fain
    Under the wintry skies to marry?

www.ingramcontent.com/pod-product-compliance
Lightning Source LLC
Chambersburg PA
CBHW020308170426
43202CB00008B/543